From Bondi Beach to Bexley ████
wall has been left unsearched ████
this brand new collection of th████
best graffiti. The choicest scri████
have been selected and introd████
Nigel Rees, author of the previous four
best-selling books in a world-famous
series. Special to this volume is a
fascinating look at graffiti in the Soviet
Union, where banishment to a Siberian
labour camp can be a very real
disincentive to the Russian Kilroy.

'Graffiti is for people who can't write
books' comments an anonymous
contributor to *Graffiti 5* — but that does
not mean they can't end up in one!

Graffiti 5 — a must for all fans of wit on
walls.

G000069455

Also by Nigel Rees in
Unwin Paperbacks

Babes and Sucklings
Eavesdroppings
Foot in Mouth
Graffiti 1
Graffiti 2
Graffiti 3
Graffiti 4
The Nigel Rees Book of
Slogans & Catchphrases
Quote ... Unquote
Quote ... Unquote 2
Quote ... Unquote 3

GRAFFITI

5

NIGEL REES

London
UNWIN PAPERBACKS
Boston   Sydney

First published in Unwin Paperbacks 1986

This book is copyright under the Berne
Convention. No reproduction without
permission. All rights reserved.

UNWIN ® PAPERBACKS
40 Museum Street, London WC1A 1LU, UK

Unwin Paperbacks,
Park Lane,
Hemel Hempstead, Herts HP2 4TE, UK

Allen & Unwin Australia Pty Ltd,
8 Napier Street, North Sydney, NSW 2060,
Australia

This edition
© Nigel Rees Productions Ltd, 1986

ISBN 0–04–827150 0

Printed in Great Britain by
Cox and Wyman Ltd, Reading

Preface

It is four years since the last little book in this series was published but the phenomenon continues — by which I mean the phenomenon of people coming up to me, or writing to me from all over the world, and thrusting items of graffiti they have spotted at me, as though my very life depended on it.

You will appreciate that this is a strange position for a person to be in — that of a kind of graffiti-confessor to whom people turn in order to get something off their chests. One such person (female) writes: 'Why do I spend so much time in the toilets of New Zealand? I guess it's because I am now a dedicated graffiti-hunter. I am addicted to graffiti. Every time I pass a public convenience, I get this urge to pop in and see if anyone has written up anything interesting. Perhaps I need help!'

I listen patiently, of course, even if like a priest I have heard it all (or most of it) before. The fact is that very little graffiti is original (or indeed very amusing or intelligent) but every spotter thinks that what he has come across is unique and brilliant.

I see my role as simply that of editor, passing on to a wider audience the pick of the mural musings, though there are those who would wish me to assume the mantle of graffiti guru. I am assumed to be permanently on the look-out for examples, wandering the world with magnifying glass and notebook in hand, as is shown by the message written on a graffiti-strewn wall in Cambridge. A large arrow drew attention to one little scribble, down at the bottom, with the comment:

HERE'S A GOOD ONE, NIGE!

Others, equally fascinated by the role that has been thrust upon me, concern themselves with the copyright question. I am told that in a ladies' loo in Australia during the 'debate' between environmentalists and the Tasmanian Government over the building of a dam on the River Franklin, someone wrote the elaborate graffito:

TO TASSIE,
FRANKLIN, MY DEAR, I DON'T GIVE A DAM

— and rounded it off with the helpful note, or warning:

(Nigel Rees — this is copyright).

Would that it were as easy as that. There is no copyright in folklore. How could there be? It is even harder to say who originated a piece of graffiti than it is to say who first invented a joke. But I'm resigned to being castigated on this score. Graffiti-writers are, of course, perfectly at liberty to put their names and addresses together with a copyright sign at the end of their work. They may, however, find that the boys in blue take rather more interest than I do.

I hesitate to make a recommendation this time as to where to go to *avoid* graffiti, though an official of the Esperanto-Asocio de Britujo assures me that he has never seen any written in Esperanto. So anti-graffitists may like to take their holidays there.

As before, I have been aided in compiling this little book not only by the creators of the graffiti quoted but also by an enthusiastic band of spotters 'from more than one country of origin' (as they say on packets of

"I used to be just a vandal but now I
write books for Nigel Rees."

orange juice). Among friends and colleagues in radio and television, Ken Bruce, Celia Haddon, Frank Delaney, Jane Glover, the late Dickie Henderson, and Paula Yates, have at one time or another sidled up and whispered graffiti in my ear. I should also mention again the member of the Shadow Cabinet with a sense of humour. Linda Baxter undertook the German translations. Among my correspondents, may I thank the following for their most welcome contributions:

P. S. Smith, Harston, Cambs.;
Andrew D. Bracey, South Ruislip, London;
Alan D. Wirdnam, Pratteln, Switzerland;
Mr & Mrs A. Joynson, Tamworth, Staffs.;
Alison Levy, Bedford Park, London;
Allan Robinson, Polegate, E. Sussex;
A. R. Burrett, Amsterdam, The Netherlands;
Amirapu Sukerna, Orissa, India;
Antero Tammisto, Helsinki, Finland;
Dr Adi Wimmer, Klagenfurt, Austria;
Bruce M. Adkins, Gif-sur-Yvette, France;
Brian Robson, Bondi, New South Wales;
Brian Corbett, Brisbane, Queensland;
Bob Shand, Leeds, W. Yorks.;
Bob Thacker, Mansfield, Notts.;
Roger J. Angus, Wellington, New Zealand;
Colin Huggett, Sheffield, S. Yorks.;
Christina Hunns, Heston, Middlesex;
Charles Stephen, Cupar, Fife;
C. V. Cherns, Pinner, London;
'Beelzebub Donkey-Scabs', Tyne and Wear;
Desmond Green, Gaborone, Botswana;
Don Hall, Sanderstead, London;
D. M. Cook, Yarm, Cleveland;
Darron M. Wilson, Alloa, Clackmannanshire;

David Pritchard, Worksop, Notts.;
Jos Meijers, Maastricht, The Netherlands;
Laurence Ekblom, Woodford Green, London;
E. T. Russell, Chingford, Essex;
Fred Scaife, Knottingley, W. Yorks;
Giles Watson, Southport, Merseyside;
Miss H. Purvis, Newbury, Berks.;
Howard Rootkin, Solihull, W. Midlands;
Jan Bastiaenssens, Ekeren, Belgium;
Jonathan Causer, Blackheath, London;
James Darwell, Bolton, Gt. Manchester;
Jack Dixon, Winnipeg, Manitoba;
John Hayday, Exeter, Devon;
Janette L. Beard, Caringbah, New South Wales;
John M. Freeman, Hong Kong;
John Shea, Surbiton, London;
J. M. Sexton, Warwick;
John Richard Dadson, Loughton, Essex;
John Watt, Hebden Bridge, W. Yorks;
Kevin Cook, Nijmegen, The Netherlands;
Kate Goldfarb, Leicester;
Kevin O'Malley, Hayes, Kent;
Lucy Fisher, Egham, Surrey;
Mrs M. Airey, Preston, Lancs.;
Mat Coward, Hampstead, London;
Miss M. H. Forrester, Leatherhead, Surrey;
Miss J. M. Markell, Mudeford, Dorset;
M. Lindsay Lambert, Ottawa, Ontario;
Ms Priya Adarkar, Bombay, India;
Margaret Walsh, Auckland, New Zealand;
Neville Gurnhill, Skegness, Lincs.;
P. A. Hanson, Fareham, Hants.;
Philip A. Rickman, Erith, Kent;
Paul M. Morrison, Wigan, Gt. Manchester;
Philip Sinclair, Bromsgrove, Heref. & Worcs.;

Paul Smith, Sheffield, S. Yorks.;
Ron Blackhouse, Worsley, Gt. Manchester;
R. J. & G. Talbott, Melton Mowbray, Leics.;
Robert McWatt, Horsforth, W. Yorks;
Richard Murch, Bermuda;
Richard Mahony, Sale, Gt. Manchester;
Stephen Burke, Oxford, Oxon;
Steve Wain, Orpington, Kent;
S. Grier, Edmonton, Alberta;
Susan Hall, Heywood, Gt. Manchester;
Tim Denes, Mosman, New South Wales;
Thalia D. Campbell, Aberystwyth, Dyfed;
Tim Harris, Bath, Avon.;
Tyler Wilson Spafford, Saint Etiennes du Gres,
France;
Valerie Knott, Northampton;
Michael Easther, Hamilton, New Zealand

... plus several Anons. and anyone I have missed out
accidentally.

I am grateful to the following for permission to
reproduce photographs and cartoons:

Churchill's 'V' sign: Photo Source
John M. Freeman;
Ken Pyne;
Nick Newman;
Tony Husband.

Where a place-name is given after a piece of graffiti,
this denotes either where the graffito was actually
seen or, if I do not have that information, the place
from which it was sent to me.
Where two separate hands have created a graffito,

this is indicated by upper and lower case settings, with the addition preceded by a dash, viz.:

HERBIE LOVES RUBY
— No he doesn't.

on bridge, Paddington, London

And, on that note, wondering who wrote the denial — Herbie? Ruby? or a third party? — let us cast off into GRAFFITI 5.

Nancy Reagan has had a face-lift.
Joan Collins uses a fork-lift.

Covent Garden, London

Joan Collins has discovered the secret of
eternal middle age.

Blackpool

If you've got water on the knee, you're not
aiming straight.

Sydney, New South Wales

TRY YOGA
— They did, and the judge said: 'How did you get
into this awful position, and look me straight in
the feet when I'm talking to you!'

Exeter

Little Miss Muffet
Sat on her tuffet
So nobody could get at it.
Along came a spider
And sat down beside her —
But he couldn't get at it either.

Oxford, 1966

The Grand Old Duchess of York
Swore she'd had ten thousand men!
She had marched them all up
To the top of the hill —
Then said, 'Go on, do it again!'

Oxford, 1966

A WOMAN'S PLACE
IS IN THE WHITE HOUSE

—Kitchen

*New York, NY, during 1984
presidential election*

Nostradamus was here, next week.
Alloa, Clackmannanshire

Ligaleiz Erdbeereis.
(Legalise strawberry ice-cream.)
West Germany

I make love like a penguin. Once a year.
Blundellsands, Merseyside

The Americans may have called them
Goons, but the Vietcong rule Ho Che *Min*.
Manchester

Clouseau Fans Against The Beumb.
London WC1, (also on badge)

CO-OP MARGARINE WORKS
— Not half as good as Vaseline.
Irlam, Gt. Manchester

Crime isn't black and white — it's various shades of Kray.
St Leonards, East Sussex (also on badge)

Judge Jeffries — was he a hanging basket or the last of the big suspenders?
Woodford Green, Gt. London

Save pipers ash

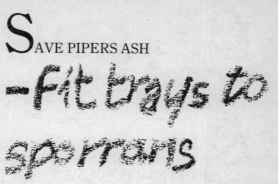

Pipers Ash, North Staffs.

Wear your puppy with pride.

Plymouth

Arise ye ungood proles from your tvs. You are watching big brother.

*by the tracks into Paddington
Station, London*

LaB mich dein Labello sein.
(Let me be your Labello.[1])

West Germany

SLIPPERY WHEN WET

— So is mine.

addition to road sign, Western Australia

THIS FOUNDATION STONE WAS LAID BY COUNCILLOR ALBERT HIGGINSON ON JULY 3RD 1897
— Please contribute generously to the Higginson Anal Repair Fund.

Bolton, Gt. Manchester

---

[1] Brand name of lipsalve.

Being Russian means never having to say you're sorry.

US, after shooting down of Korean airliner, 1983

Vote Labour and fight truth decay.

Ruislip, London

Graffiti in Transit

Written in the dust on the back of vehicles, or on car-stickers, or both ...

(on a Mini:)

This was a Rolls before it went through the carwash.

This is the F-Plan car. It goes like the wind.

Life begins at 40 mph.

You've heard of the Flying Dutchman? Well, I am the Flying Irishman. And how do you like my plane?

When I set off I had a water-skier behind me.

HGV – Heavy Groping Vehicle.

I got the keys for this car at a wife-swapping party.

I lost it at the carwash.

M OT – Miles of trouble.

N o hand signals. They're busy.

I am a member of the Yard High Club.

Sex is evil
Sex is sin
Sex is forgiven
So sex is in.

bus station, Northampton

Sex is Sin
Sin is in
So open your legs
And let me in.

Brisbane, Queensland

Q. Which are more popular — chickens or owls?

A. Chickens! Have you ever heard of Kentucky Fried Owls?

New Barnet

Save *EastEnders* — Act now.
BBC TV studios, Elstree

This space donated by the silent majority.
*on blank wall awaiting new
advertisements, London Underground*

I'm immortal. So far.
Maidstone (also on badge)

Ashes to ashes
Dust to dust
If it wasn't for you
My cock would rust.
*girls' loo, Penrose High School,
Auckland, New Zealand*

HEAVY PLANT CROSSING
— Bloddibiguss Jaycebeeii.

Wigan

(On notice of the memorial service for Lord Howard of Henderskelfe, the kaftan-wearing former Chairman of the BBC, in December 1984:)

Please Bring Bottle and Bird.

London W1

If you laid the Chinese end to end around the world, do you know that you'd drown half the buggers?
— BROODY ENGRISH!

Bolton

Racists go home.

Maastricht, The Netherlands

Vote reagan –
NOT FRITZ AND TITZ.

US, 1984 (also on badge)

Susan Green is just like Junction 21 on the
M1. The Leicester TURN-OFF.

motorway service area on M1

Happiness is driving over a
TRAFFIC WARDEN.

in dust on lorry seen on A606

There's more hops in a dead frog than in a pint of Ben Truman.

Catworth, Cambs.

Even Hitler was afraid of the Methodists.

remote loo in North East Scotland

What's pink and hard and comes in the morning? The FT crossword.

London NW1

Don't stand for sexual harassment in the office — lie on the desk.

Skegness

Napoleon wore his sleeve on his heart.

Oxford

---

*(Next to a series of rivets on lavatory partition,
Leeds School of Dentistry:)*

For our blind readers.

THOMAS WHITELEY
(1904–68)

cemetery, Headingley, W. Yorks.

(Under an advert for TV Times *showing* Crossroads *character Adam Chance ogling a female:)*

GIVE PEACE A CHANCE – JOHN LENNON.
GIVE CHANCE A PIECE – ADAM CHANCE.

Leeds

If you take a shower with your clothes on, it shows you're mad. If you take a shower with your clothes off, it shows your nuts.

Erith, Kent

Bi-sexuals get twice as much fun.

Ilkley

Land Rights for Gay Whales

Sydney, New South Wales[1]

When Mary had a little lamb
The doctor was surprised.
But when Old MacDonald had a farm
He couldn't believe his eyes.

University of Sydney

CHELSEA RULE OK
— Whereas Cambridge United exhibit traits
indicative of inherent superiority.

Cambridge football ground

[1] According to the *Dictionary of Australian Quotations*
(Heinemann, 1984), this slogan for the ultimate cause was originated
by Margaret Roadknight in a revue at Adelaide in 1979.

The Irish don't know what they want and won't be happy till they get it.

various military locations in the UK

Why are there only nineteen letters in the alphabet?
ET went home,
JR got shot,
the angels sang no L,
the B buzzed off,
and the P is running down your leg.

school, Birmingham

We may not have ivy-covered walls but there's something strange growing up the sides of the genetics department.

University of Sheffield

To hold down the people forever is like holding up a hand to the sun.

El Salvador, 1981

(Added to the name of a station on the London Underground:)

POSTERLEY **for Christmas**

How do we know that Jesus was a Jew?
1. He lived at home till he was thirty.
2. He went into his father's business.
3. His mother thought he was the Messiah.
4. He thought his mother was a virgin.

New Barnet

When God gave brains, I thought he said trains, so I asked for a small, slow one.

Birmingham (also on badge)

Aufwiedersprayen

Pratteln, Switzerland, after graffiti had been removed by the town council

Mehr Wahlium fur das Volk.
(More Valium for the People.)

Pratteln, Switzerland

My wife's into S & M — snoring and moaning.

London W2

Did you hear about the gynaecologist who papered the hall through the letterbox?

Fulham, London

SAVE PLANKTON – KILL THE WHALE!

University of Sydney

Sandy Gall's got a nerve

London W1

(During the ITV showing of the sci-fi series V, 1984:)

'V' have vays of making you miss the Olympics.

Alloa

Who took the fizz out of physics? The same twit who took the mystery out of chemistry.

Exeter

Noddy has Big Ears.

Cambridge

My friend's friend is his enema.

London WC2

Q. What's hairy and got six sides?

A. A pubic cube.

Newcastle-upon-Tyne

Oral sex — a taste of things to come?

Manchester

Don't take the piss out of Wilson's [ale] — it needs all the flavour it can get.

traditional

Computers rule 10110101 11100101

Bermuda

I'M NOT AS THUNK AS DRINKLE PEOPLE PEEP I AM.

Brighton (also on badge)[1]

---

[1] As a quotation in the form, 'I'm not so think as you drunk I am,' this is from the 'Ballad of Soporific Absorption' by Sir John Squire (1884–1958), the poet, essayist and critic.

Q. What does it take to circumcise a whale?

A. Four skin divers.

*women's lavatory,
University of Winnipeg*

Are angry dolphins at cross porpoises?

London NW1

There are fairy-cakes at the bottom of our garden.

on side of bakery, Alloa

Don't bother about Moss Bros — the Hackney Robbery Squad will fit you up.

Knightsbridge Crown Court, London

Go on, gi'us a wash.
in dirt on car, London NW1

Gone to work — back in ten minutes.
on back of lavatory door, Sydney

Arthur Scargill is a miner offence.
Leeds

I LIKE WRITING ON WALLS
— This is a door, you fool.
*loo door, Palmerston North, New
Zealand*

ALL POLICEMEN ARE BASTARDS

—But some have birth certificates which show that they ain't —Clever bastards.

Solihull

(On poster advertising Royal Academy Summer Exhibition:)

With English subtitles.

London SW1

I love cricket – you should see my overnight stand.

Brighton

WHAT DOES JESUS OFFER?
– 2 Cs and a D to princes.

*Cambridge, 1983, on entry of Prince
Edward to Jesus College*

Old soldiers never die – just their privates.

traditional

Avenge yourself. Live long enough to be a problem to your kids.

on van on M5 near Taunton

S hergar[1] is alive and well and living under an assumed mane.

Dublin, 1983

S hergar please phone home.

Wales, 1983

V ISIT CLUB MED MURAROA
— And have a real blast!

Auckland, New Zealand

Love is an empty jam-jar

Amsterdam

---

[1] Shergar, the champion race-horse, was stolen from a stud farm in Ireland and never recovered.

A.C.A.B.[1]

traditional

Q. Why is Mrs Thatcher like a toilet?

A. Because she gets rid of jobs.

Camden Town, London, 1983

Here's to the breezes
That blow past little girls' kneezes
And up to the spot
Which teases and pleases
And causes diseases.

*University of Victoria,
Victoria, BC*

---

[1] 'All Coppers Are Bastards.'

E quality rarely breeds quality.

London WC1

J oan Collins makes a movie a year. She's just started her 67th.

Birmingham

I f Typhoo put the T in Britain, who put the Arse in Arsenal?

Erith station, Kent

S upport the Irish hunger strikers. Send them food parcels.

University of Sydney

Val Doonican has gone off his rocker.

Skegness

The Pope likes Valley Girls.

US, 1983

STOPERA.

*by opponents of opera
house complex,
Amsterdam*

Q. What do kangaroos and vibrators have
in common?
A. They're both in the meat substitution
business.

Melbourne

P.L.O. GO HOME.

Notting Hill, London

Men are like lavatories — they're either engaged or full of shit.

women's lavatory, Hampstead, London

MY DADDY LOVES MY MUMMY

in childish hand, on sea wall at Broadstairs

Q. What is the difference between herpes and true love?

A. Herpes lasts forever.

New York, New York

I LIKE IT BUT NOT THEM

in lipstick in women's loo, Wales

E.T. – phone home.
E.T. – call Carl Sagan.

Wellington, New Zealand

E.T. Go Home.

Auckland, New Zealand

E.T. has herpes.

Los Angeles, 1983

DRACULA'S SCHOOL REPORT:
Reading — Good.
Writing — Fair.
Cricket — Has the makings of a good bat.

Salford

Dear George — Moscow Rules OK.

Cheltenham, 1982

Hungarian wines rule Tokay.

Bombay

Say it with flowers — send a triffid.

Catworth, Cambs.

Trix is nix.

The government is up to its trix again.

Geen bekroning zonder woning.
[NO CROWNING WITHOUT HOUSING.]

*all from Amsterdam at time of
crowning of Queen Beatrix, 1980*

Snow White knew all about Seven-Up *before*
she discovered Smirnoff.
(signed)
Droopy.

Preston

Narcissus fancies himself.

Alloa

When we're right nobody remembers.
When we're wrong nobody forgets.

gents' loo, North Shore, Auckland

4 ever
2 gever
4 years
2 cum.

Erith, Kent

Black is beautiful, but unemployed.

US, 1983

Who says I'm paranoid? And why do they want to know?

University of Sydney

If it's going on, it's going in. [1]

on contraceptive vending machine,
Glasgow

FREE THE BEETHOVEN 9

at pub used by musicians of the
Amsterdam Concertgebouw

---

[1] A slogan of the *Sunday Mail*.

Ban S & M — stop beating about the bush!
Tullamarine airport, Melbourne

None but the brave deserve the fare.
Leeds, 1980, on announcement of bus fares increase

Emunctory snot what it used to be!
Solihull

The Irish use two contraceptives, to be sure, to be sure.
Peterborough

EVE WAS FRAMED
— I get the picture
    (signed)
        Adam.

Exeter

Next to my mother-in-law, this is the best shithouse I know!

gents' loo, youth hostel, Scotland

Q. What's old and wrinkled and hangs out
    your trousers?
A. Your mother.

Railway Square, Sydney

Come in 'Mary Rose', your time is up!

near Portsmouth dockyard, 1982

Rangers rule.

Sloane Square tube station, London

A Merry Xmas to All Our Raiders.

*written in dirt on back of police
mini-bus in Coventry just before
Christmas 1984*

OUTSIDE OF WALL

*on wall by tracks at
Marylebone station, London 1984*

Where are all these Guards at 4/9 for 20?

*Salisbury pub, St Martins Lane,
London, 1964*

Stand closer, your Grace, the next nobleman may have bare feet.

gents, Arundel Castle

A woman who seeks to be equal with men lacks ambition.

Tucson, Arizona

Italy has more elections than a Chink on his honeymoon.

Manchester

Arthur Scargill has moles in his pits.

Bath

I wos 'ere
'Ere I woz
Woz I 'ere?
'Course I woz!

Southampton

Van Gogh woz ear

Kemnay, Inverurie, Aberdeenshire

I like blondes. They get dirty quicker.

Fetternear, Aberdeenshire

I've read so much about the dangers of drinking and smoking that I've decided to give up reading.

Barford, Norfolk

Some come here to sit and think
Some come here to shit and stink
Some come here to wash their balls —
But I come here to read the walls!

Mudeford, Dorset

There once was a young man called Stensil
Whose prick was as sharp as a pencil.
He punctured an actress
Two sheets and a mattress
And dented the bedroom utensil.

traditional

Close encounters of the thud kind.

*on notice advertising programme on
meteors and meteorites at
planetarium in Wellington, New
Zealand*

I like knee-tremblers. The earth always moves for me.

Aston Clinton, Bucks.

Q. What's a Hindu?
A. Lays eggs.

Newcastle-upon-Tyne

Marriage isn't a word but a sentence.

Newhaven

Love is like a photograph ... it develops in the dark.

University of Sydney

Nieder mit dem Fahrstuhl.
[Down with the lift.]

West Germany

What do you get when you send a Joan Collins dress to an African laundry? Cinzano on the rocks.

Moulsford, Oxon.

Joan Collins can pour it over me any time.

Newtown, Powys

Keep the Pope off the moon! It's the only place he hasn't been.

Kirkby, Merseyside

V

OTEZ EXTREME CENTRE.

Paris, 1981

N

ew Year is cancelled — they've found the old one.

Leicester

V

AN DYCK IS A LESBIAN TRUCK DRIVER.

Covent Garden, London

NO TO BOTHA. YES TO BOTHAM.

North London

(Inscription alleged to have been found on an ancient earthenware receptacle thrown up by a bomb blast during World War Two:)

I TIS APIS SPOTANDA FINEO NE.
Valletta, Malta

M agic rules — hocus pocus.
Bombay

I thought the AA was a motoring organisation until I discovered Smirnoff.
Oxford

A rt is what you can get away with.
Walker Art Gallery, Liverpool

I used to think A10 was the road to Cambridge until I discovered a crate of Smirnoff in my locker.

Knightsbridge Crown Court
(A10 is the section of Scotland
Yard which investigates complaints
against the police)

Practise artificial insemination — keep your hand in.

Weston-super-Mare

NO ONE DOES IT BETTER THAN ME

— where can I contact no one?

Alloa

T he Ayatollah is uncircumcised. There's no
end to the prick.

Sydney

$$B \ 4\sqrt[1]{U} \ \frac{RU}{18}$$

- LIM!
- RUL!
- L. IM 22.
- O, OK.

University of Sheffield

R EAD BEDE.

New College, Oxford

B estiality — 9 out of 10 cats said their owners
preferred it.

London W1

I knew Elizabeth Taylor when she didn't know
where her next husband was coming from.

New York, NY

T HE BISHOP OF DURHAM KNOWS
WHAT HE IS DOING.
— That's what scares me.

outside Berkshire church

I'VE GOT HERMES
— SURELY YOU MEAN 'HERPES'?
— NO, I'M THE CARRIER!

Carlisle

Abigamist is an Italian fog.

Southampton

Beneath the spreading chestnut tree
The village idiot sat,
Amusing himself
By abusing himself
And catching it all in his hat.

Chicago

BLAIR PEACH IS ALIVE AND WELL AND
LIVING IN AN ORCHARD IN NEW ZEALAND
— No! that's Blair Rabbit!
— No! that's Blair Labbit who lives in China.
Knightsbridge Crown Court, London

My girlfriend can't wrestle, but you should
see her box.
Flinders Street Station, Melbourne

Capitalism is the survival of the fattest.
University of Sheffield

Linda Lovelace has gone down in my
estimation.
London SE1

I left my heart in El Salvador (and my head).

US, 1983

Constipation means never having to give a shit.

Dallas, Tex.

THE RETURN OF JULIAN BREAM
— just when you thought it was safe to go to the lute.

on poster, Amsterdam

FREE THE UB40

Harlow, Essex

IF YOU *NOTICE* THIS
NOTICE YOU WILL
NOTICE THAT THIS
NOTICE IS NOT WORTH
NOTICING.
SO DON'T NOTICE IT.

University of Sydney

Steve McGarrett rules Hawaii-FIVE-OK?

Ipswich

CUNT'S
— You thick bastard, you don't have an
apostrophe there.
— Speak for yourself — you haven't seen MINE!

Egham, Surrey

First we were a kingdom under a king, then an empire under an emperor, now we're a country under Maggie Thatcher.

Seaforth, Merseyside

My wife has two cunts. I'm one of them.

Birmingham

Is instant curry just a flash in the pan?

Harston, Cambs.

Diarrhoea is hereditary — it runs in your jeans.

Oxford

WHAT CAN A DICK DO THAT A BIG BANANA CAN'T?

— Go limp.

Carlton, Victoria

YOU CRIED FOR MARK, MAGGIE.
St Helen's, Lancs., during Falklands war, 1982 (alluding to Mrs Thatcher's earlier distress when her son had gone missing in the Trans-Sahara car rally)

Q. What's an Irish contraceptive like?
A. Hand me that ball of wool and I'll knit you one.

Baslow, Derbyshire

They're still doing it

Like the 'So-and-so rules OK' graffiti series (now all but defunct), the 'do it' theme has proved itself capable of considerable variation in recent years. Here are some more of the doings:

Divers do it deeper.

Civil servants do it in a minute.

Elevator men do it up and down.

L umberjacks do it with their little choppers.

V iolinists fiddle around at it.

Cyclists have it between their legs

A stronomers do it with a collapsible instrument.

A stronomers do it with one eye open.

Teachers do it with class.

Publishers do it between covers.

Booksellers do it over the counter

Marathon runners keep it up for hours.

Chinese food lovers want to do it again twenty minutes afterwards.

Bartenders do it on the rocks.

Hang-gliders stay up longer.

Missionaries do it on their knees.

Politicians just talk about it.

The House of Commons can't do it in one sitting.

George does it Best.

Paris has to get plastered to do it.

Donyatt Dog Club does it with discipline and kindness.

Water-skiers do it behind boats.

Hancockians do it H-H-Half-Hourly.

Morticians are dead keen on it.

Skiers go down faster.

Farmers do it in wellies.

Torvill and Dean do it on thin ice.

Footballers do it in the bath afterwards.

S kiers do it with both legs together.

G ordon does it in a Flash.

C alligraphers do it at forty-five degrees.

T he Treorchy Male Voice Choir does it all
through the night.

all the above from various
sources

Linguists do it orally.
Karajan does it with a little stick.
Fencers don't do it — they feint.
Epistemologists do it knowingly.
Historians do it looking back.

all from Klagenfurt, Austria

Yorkies are made in York. Good job they're not made in Goole.

York

Q. What's the difference between LA and yoghurt?
A. Yoghurt is a live culture.

Los Angeles, California

To ERR IS HUMMAN.

Brisbane, Queensland

Down with the nodding dogs of capitalism.

in dirt on car, Bexleyheath, London

L OW DOOR – DUCK

– Or grouse

on notice in half-timbered building, Wiltshire

S IT ON A HAPPY FACE.

Detroit

J OHN LENNON LIVES
– No wonder I can't get the bloody will probated
(signed)
Yoko Ono.

Leeds, 1981

If you don't smoke, I won't fart.

Sydney

Do lesbians enjoy a little bit of
'How's-your-mother'?

Hamilton, New Zealand

Have a fart — you know it make scents.

Covent Garden

Dr Finlay, Dr Finlay, I've got heartburn.
Shut up Janet, and take your tit out of the
porridge.

London N1

Behind every successful man is a fish with a
bicycle.

Ottawa

Go into genetics and get ahead (or two).

University of Sheffield

PUNKS NOT DEAD

Punktuation is

West Wickham station, Kent

J ESUS SAVES
– Religiously.

Exeter

M y graffiti are killing me.

Newbury

Graffiti is for people who can't write books.

London W1

(In a lavatory cubicle:)

This is a fast checkout for people with seven items or less.

Doncaster

To the fellow who drew on this wall:
Sir, your mind is exceedingly small.
I like not your wit,
Nor the shape of her tit,
And the balls on that bloke are too small.

Aldershot

I just fell in love with my hand.

Liverpool

Ladies — want something hot, red and throbbing between your legs?
Ride a Honda.

Melbourne

Turner painted skies by nimbus.

Cambridge

'V' Haff Ways of
Making You Chalk

The 'V for Victory' slogan of the Second World War was expressed in several ways. The opening three notes of Beethoven's Fifth Symphony corresponded to the (... —) of the 'V' in Morse Code and, accordingly, the music was used in BBC broadcasts to occupied Europe.

People gave the 'V for Victory' salute with parted middle index fingers (though Winston Churchill confused matters by presenting his fingers the wrong way round in a manner akin to the traditionally obscene gesture).

To start with, though, the 'V' was a coded graffiti slogan, inscribed on walls in occupied Belgium by members of the anti-German 'freedom movement'. The Flemish word for freedom begins with a V — *Vrijheid* — and the French word for victory is, of course, *Victoire*. The idea came from Victor de Laveleye, the BBC's Belgian Programme Organiser, who, in a broadcast on 14 January 1941, suggested that

listeners should adopt the letter 'V' as 'a symbol of their belief in the ultimate victory of the allies'.[1] They were to go out and chalk it up wherever they could.

From Belgium, the idea spread into the Netherlands and France and 'multitudes' of little Vs started appearing on walls in those countries. In a BBC English-language broadcast to resistance workers in Europe on 31 July 1941, 'Colonel Britton' (Douglas Ritchie) said:

It's about the V — the sign of victory — that I want to talk to you now. All over Europe the V sign is seen by the Germans and to the Germans and the Quislings it is indeed the writing on the wall. It is the sign which tells them that one of the unknown soldiers has passed that way. And it's beginning to play on their nerves.

They see it chalked on pavements, pencilled on posters, scratched on the mudguards of German cars. Flowers come up in the shape of a V; men salute each other with the V sign separating their fingers. The number five is a V and men working in the fields turn to the village clocks as the chimes sound the hour of five.

---

[1] Gerard Mansell, *Let Truth Be Told* (Weidenfeld & Nicolson, 1982).

The 'Colonel' also encouraged the use of the V sound — three short taps and a heavy one:

> When you knock on a door, there's your knock. If you call a waiter in a restaurant, call him like this: 'Eh, garçon!' (*taps rhythm on wine glass*) ... Tell all your friends about it and teach them the V sound. If you and your friends are in a cafe and a German comes in, tap out the V sign all together.

From these broadcasts emerged the evocative slogan. 'The night is your friend, the "V" is your sign'.

Winston Churchill spoke of the 'V' sign as a symbol of 'the unconquerable will of the people of the occupied territories'.

The 'V for Victory' theme became a potent part of the folklore of the Second World War ... and it all began as a piece of officially-encouraged graffiti.

JESUS IS COMING
— And Mary Magdalene is breathing hard.
Newcastle Polytechnic

Q. What's the connection between
Captain Kirk and Jeremy Thorpe?
A. They both want more thrust off Scotty.
Manchester, 1979

Princess Anne for Mare.

Cambridge

Life is like a penis — when it's hard you get
fucked, when it's soft you can't beat it.
Princeton, New Jersey

Q. Senator Kennedy, what would you do to strengthen the economy?

A. Let's drive off that bridge when we come to it.

Experience the joy of giving and receiving — masturbate.

Knoxville, Tennessee

He who knows but knows not that he knows, is asleep.   Wake him.
He who knows not and knows not that he knows not, can be taught.   Teach him.
He who knows not but thinks that he knows, is a fool.   Avoid him.
He who knows and knows that he knows, is a prophet.   Follow him.

pub, Leeds

Acorns rule oak, eh?

on tree, Tamworth

If you voted National last election, you can't shit here — your arse-hole's in Wellington.

in loo on ferry-boat between Auckland and Waiheke Island, New Zealand, 1983

We demand: Away with the Alps — unrestricted view of the Mediterranean!

West Germany

Beware Scott of the arse-antics.

Knightsbridge Crown Court, at the time of the Jeremy Thorpe case

There was a young man from South Ken
Who fancied disabled young men.
From positions strategic
Each guy paraplegic
Was serviced and wheeled out again.

Covent Garden, London

WHERE WOULD FASHION BE
WITHOUT PINS?
— Free of little pricks.

on ad for Pretty Polly stockings,
Turnham Green, London

Square seats don't seem to bother 'em,
They've got some rum bums in Rotherham.

gents' loo, Rotherham railway
station, where seats did indeed
used to be square (once quoted by
Stanley Baldwin)

Q. What's long and hard and has semen in it?

A. No, a submarine.

Hobart, Tasmania

SEX INSTRUCTOR — First Lesson Free.

on lorry on M27

Three chairs for Cyril Smith

St Helens

There are so many beautiful women in Amsterdam — what a pity none of them speaks Dutch.

translated from the Dutch

Nymphomaniacal Alice
Used TNT instead of a phallus.
They found her vagina
In South Carolina
And her bumhole in Buckingham Palace.

traditional

If you find out who is shagging my mistress I'll
shoot his guide dog.

Knightsbridge Crown Court, London

The living are just the dead on holiday.

Brighton[1]

[1] A quotation from Maurice Maeterlinck (1862–1949), the Belgian poet and dramatist.

THE EARTH SUCKS
— Is that why boys lie face down when
sunbathing?

Bondi, NSW

If you knew Suzie
Like I know Suzie
I'd beat your friggin head in.

University of Sheffield

Don't vote, do it yourself.

London W11

Sex is just one damp thing after another.

Felixstowe

74% SAY NO

— And 26% get Pregnant

addition to poster protesting
against the abolition of the
Greater London Council, 1985

M

Y WILLY IS BIG
— Mine is small but often used.
— Mine varies according to the occasion.

University of Warwick

Q.

What does Barbara Woodhouse say
when she wants a dog to do its
business?

A.   ****!

Yarm, Cleveland

ELVIS IS DEAD
— Good career move!

New York, NY

Here I sit and contemplate —
Should I shit or masturbate?

Melbourne

BARBARA WOODHOUSE DRIVES A
SIT-RON.

Bootle

Cheese is the stuff dreams are made of.

Solihull

I muddled get my words sometimes up.

Alloa

T he first wearer of your fur coat died in it.

Carshalton, 1978

W ill the real Lazarus please stand up!

London W11

GODOT MUST HAVE USED
PUBLIC TRANSPORT.

University of Sydney

I ought to have an inferiority complex but I haven't.

University of Sheffield

D id you know Marjorie Proops?

Imperial College, London

J oan Collins is a former has-been.

Barnet, London

I feel like a new woman and I only came in to have my prostate removed.

hospital, Leicester

As you get fat, it becomes difficult to avoid a speeding bus. And as you grow fatter, it becomes even more difficult for the bus to avoid you.

on slimming parlour, Orissa, India

WHY DO SKINHEADS BUY THEIR BRACES FROM TIMOTHY WHITES? BECAUSE THEY DON'T WANT TO BOVVER BOOTS.

Leicester

NOBODY KNOWS WHERE MY JOHNNY HAS GONE[1]
— Wanna borrow one of mine?

Birkenhead

---

[1] Line from the song 'It's My Party'.

Can I kaja you googoos?

Dagenham

If the £50 you can afford,
    Then go ahead and pull the cord.
If the £50 you do not own,
    Then leave the fucking thing alone.

next to train communication cord

Chalk Marx

Graffiti does not exist in the Soviet Union.
Indeed, if you believe that the examples which
follow ever appeared on Soviet walls, you are
quite clearly a subversive and, like the people
who put them there, liable to find yourself
enjoying a long stay in a Siberian labour camp!

Until Arthur Hawes and Ivan Ivanovitch
Zapiskin returned with the collection from which
these examples are taken, I was under the
impression that very few graffiti were to be found
in the Soviet Union because the odds stacked
against Ivan Kilroys were so formidable. They
have to write in chalk because felt-tipped pens
and spray paint are not available. They cannot
even rely on the privacy of a lavatory cubicle to
work in: the main gents' lavatories tend not to
have doors. And, as there is no advertising apart
from official slogans, they are denied the
inspiration of — and writing surface for — so
much Western graffiti.

Yet in spite of these obstacles and the
draconian penalties meted out to those who do
try to overcome them, 'backfence literature' *does*
exist in the Soviet Union. Indeed, it can be

argued that, in a country where the only communications allowed are official ones, graffiti are an important alternative mode of expression. Certainly, they appear to reflect the same laconic view of life and of the authorities that comes through underground jokes of the 'Radio Armenia' variety.

It is ironic that the Soviet system should rely so much on political sloganeering and go to such lengths to stamp out relatively harmless wall-writing. Not that all Soviet graffiti are politically inclined. Not even the KGB has managed to find a way of clamping down on jokes of an extremely earthy lavatorial and sexual nature.

What follows has been assembled from several Soviet cities, including Moscow, Leningrad, Viborg, Kiev, Minsk, Tashkent and Tbilisi. Messrs Hawes and Zapiskin — these are not their real names — assembled their collection during three visits in the early 1980s. Quite how they managed to slip out of their hotels and avoid Intourist guides must remain a secret. Looking for graffiti in the Soviet Union is markedly harder than in the West. For the reasons already given, there is less of it. Not being written in open public places, for the most part it has to be tracked down in nooks and crannies.

Occasionally, a graffito *does* get written up in a public place, but it is soon removed. The fact that it is written in chalk makes this all the easier. However, when the young Moscow dissident

'Nikolai' was charged in the early 1970s with writing graffiti over the walls at the factory where he worked, he made a rather better job of it. He used a special hard-to-remove paint to write such slogans as, 'Why is there no meat in the shops?' 'Where are our human rights?' 'Why are wages so low?' 'Why are elections fixed?' His sentence of seven years in Siberian exile presumably reflected the trouble he had given the authorities in trying to remove his handiwork.

In essence, though, his offence had been to provide written material intended for public consumption without the approval of the censor — not that graffiti would be approved anyway.

Another contrast between Russian graffiti and the type often found in the West — notably in New York — is that it is almost never found in the underground stations and trains of Moscow and Leningrad. The reasons for this must be, firstly, that vandalising the Metro can lead to extremely harsh punishments but, secondly, and more significantly, the citizens of these two places take great pride in the railway systems which are elegantly and immaculately maintained.

Another difficulty: telephone booths are covered in either a red metallic paint or corrugated aluminium which makes doodling impossible, even though long delays while waiting for a connection provide ample opportunity.

And so, life is made harder and harder for the

Russian Kilroy. But graffiti will out. He bounces back just the same, even if he is not always strong on literacy. He may have something to say but seldom spells it correctly.

A popular graffito in the West in recent years has been: 'Visit the USSR before the USSR visits you.' Before you can respond to that slogan, or before the threat becomes fact, what follows will give you a foretaste.

Except where obviously not, the graffiti have been translated from the Russian.

Why do Russians walk around in threes? So there is one who can read, one who can write, and one who can keep an eye on the two intellectuals.

Moscow graffito, attributed to a visiting Czech

Before 1917, 97% OF THE RUSSIAN POPULATION WERE ILLITERATE PEASANTS
— So what's changed?

addition to propaganda poster in a Moscow park

LENIN DIED BUT HIS WORK LIVES ON
— Better the other way round.
added to an official banner

What's a hundred metres long and eats cabbage? The queue outside a Moscow butcher's shop.

Men — Slaves of the State
Women — Slaves of Slaves.

TV IN ALL ROOMS. ONLY HERE *THEY* WATCH *YOU*.
English graffito at Cosmos Hotel,
for athletes taking part in 1980
Olympics

A hen is not a bird.
Poland is not the West.

A COCKROACH HAS A MOUSTACHE.
A BOY HAS UNDERPANTS.

I pump for tea and hope for vodka.

on tea-vending machine, Leningrad

A Russian who can chew gum and still be
free is a Russian who doesn't mince his words.

lavatory wall, Moscow, in the 1970s
(Before the 1980 Moscow Olympics,
there was no chewing gum in the
Soviet Union, so a Soviet citizen
would have had to have illegal
dealings with foreigners to procure
it.)

When the end of the world comes the only safe country will be the Soviet Union. The Soviet Union is fifty years behind the rest of the world.

BETWEEN TWO BEAUTIFUL ROSES, A TOADSTOOL MAY GROW.

The reason there's no fish in the Moscow market is so you won't notice there's no meat.

HER C*** IS AS WIDE
AS A TROUSER'S BACKSIDE,
YOU CAN SIT ON THE EDGE
AND DANGLE YOUR LEGS.

Sara died of cancer. It was her favourite position.

in Russian, 'cancer' and 'crabs' are the same word, and crab-style is the equivalent of 'doggy-style' in English

In the Soviet Union there are only three ways to enjoy yourself: first — getting drunk, second — getting drunk, and third — getting drunk.

A Soviet intellectual is he who goes directly to a loony-bin demanding right of asylum.

A MILK-MAID WILL GET YOU LAID.

If you want to get screwed — buy a car.
If you want to be a passenger — get married.

The latest Soviet fad — live black:
— holiday on the Black Sea,
— eat black caviar,
— drive a black Volga,
— deal on the black market.

> *KGB officers drive black Volgas and
> do some of the other things
> mentioned*

LONG LIVE ALL POETS PUBLISHED
UPON THESE WALLS
INSTEAD OF IN JOURNALS ON
NEWSPAPER STALLS
— In the midst of crap we are poets,
In the midst of all poets we are all crap.

> *lavatory, Tashkent airport, 1972*

New Soviet Tsar dynasty since 1917
Revolution:
  Vladimir the Wise (Lenin)
  Joseph the Terrible (Stalin)
  Nikita the Splendid (Khruschev)
  Leonid the Chronicler (Brezhnev)
  Jurij the Longhanded (Andropov)

*Moscow University — the honorifics
are those of actual Tsars in
Russian history. Jurij the
Longhanded, for example, was Tsar Jurij
Dalgoukov of the eleventh century*

Glad to be alive? No, surprised!

lavatory wall, Moscow

She can't be hugged, she can't be kissed
She's the guide from Intourist

Leningrad hotel

Below the sickle — above the hammer,
This is the seal of our Soviet banner.
Whatever in life you chose to do
It's all the same — you still get screwed.

Why is there no meat in the Soviet union?
Because the sheep work and the cows govern.

The first thing a Russian worker does after
leaving work is take his hands from his pockets.
That's why the economy has gone to hell.

Afghanistan and the Soviet Union are
brothers.
Brothers are not friends — they are chosen.

If you have any requirements, please contact Reception. We'll explain why you can't have them.

English graffito, in lavatory of
the Hotel Rossia, Moscow

'WITHIN FIVE YEARS COMMUNISM WILL OVERTAKE THE CAPITALIST WEST WHICH NOW STANDS ON THE EDGE OF A PRECIPICE' – Brezhnev.

Things may be bad but they're better than next year.

BORIS. GO HOME AT ONCE. TANIA'S IN BED WITH IVAN.

lavatory wall, Leningrad

By 1985, one Soviet citizen in every five will have a car, one in three will have a television and one in two will own a pair of socks.

lavatory wall, Moscow University

The Soviet economy is a planned economy. When there's no ham, there's no eggs.

NEW STYLE RUSSIAN ROULETTE: A MAN GOES TO BED WITH SIX WOMEN — ONE OF THEM IS A CANNIBAL.

Join the Union of Soviet Writers. Publish a book and denounce two comrades.

New trade agreement between US and USSR: 10,000 cadillacs delivered to Soviet Union in exchange for 10,000 parking spaces — in Rerezov, Siberia.

Moscow, 1979

THE POLLUTION IS TERRIBLE. IF WE WERE ALLOWED TO BREATHE WE'D BE IN TROUBLE.

outside Leningrad chemical factory

IF IT WERE NOT NECESSARY TO EAT AND WEAR CLOTHING THE SOVIET REGIME WOULD BE THE BEST IN THE WORLD.

Capitalism is the exploitation of man by man. Socialism is the opposite.

The straight line of Soviet policy.

When there's food in the villages and none in the cities — that's right wing deviationism.
When there's food in the cities and none in the villages — that's left wing deviationism.
When there's food in the cities and in the villages — that's capitalist propaganda.

Nose like a potato. Penis like a concertina.
Russian version of the ancient Greek axiom: 'He who is born with a hook nose will have a prick as strong as an oak'

F*** YOUR MOTHER
— Why a mother when you can get a goat?
lavatory wall, Tbilisi, Georgia

WHEN BREZHNEV VISITS,
EVERYONE CAN SHOW THEIR UNBRIDLED
JOY BY RATTLING THEIR CHAINS.
*Kalingrad, Lithuania (prior to a
visit by the then Soviet leader)*

ONE DAY THE USSR WILL OWN ALL
THE LAND IN THE WORLD
— Where will we put our wheat?

A trade union questionnaire:
Were you in gaol? If not, why?

Stalin was bad head of state, very bad.
Lenin was good head of state, very good.
Brezhnev? When he's dead we'll find out.

Half past five.
This means impotence because of the picture it makes on the clock face. A quarter past six is something to be happy about.

Khruschev is the first man in history to have sown grain in Siberia and harvested it in Canada.

The Soviet economy can be summarised as follows: Temporary Difficulties.

Rumours are started by the Voice of America, denied by Pravda, and finally carried out by the Soviet Government.

GIRLS! GUARD YOUR BLACK SUITCASES.

Russian metaphor for vagina

Boris used to live across the street from the Butirka prison. Now he lives across the street from his house.

A Socialist government is a government that gives a headache to all the citizens and then provides free aspirins.

A MELON RIPENS WITH THE SUN.
ARMENIANS THINK THAT BUGGERY'S
FUN.

lavatory, Moscow

A WOMAN WITHOUT A MAN IS LIKE A
FISH WITHOUT AN UMBRELLA.

*Russian version of a well-known
Western graffito (bicycles are not
common in the Soviet Union)*

U SSR survival regulations:

1. Don't think.
2. If you think, don't talk.
3. If you talk, don't write it down.
4. If you write it down, don't publish it.
5. If you publish it, don't sign it.
6. If you sign it, deny it at once.

Chinese fight with people.
Americans fight with machines.
Russians fight with propaganda.

In Russia they teach two foreign languages:
Hebrew and Chinese. Hebrew for those leaving
for Israel, Chinese for those who stay.

Brezhnev is like a crocodile — when he
opens his mouth you don't know if it's to smile or
eat someone.

Reality and miracles are interwoven.
Any prick might be Beethoven.

In Germany what is allowed is allowed
  And what is not allowed is not allowed.
In France what is allowed is allowed
  And what is not allowed is also allowed.
In Russia what is not allowed is not allowed
  And what is allowed is also not allowed.

The only thing a Russian pickpocket gets is practice.

The less we love a woman the more we are loved by her.

on a Leningrad wall (quoting Pushkin)

Don't spit on the floor. It's forbidden to discuss politics in public.

outside public lavatory, Leningrad

DREAM OF THE IMPOTENT!
*inscribed on the base of the Cosmos Statue,
Prospekt Mira, Moscow, shortly
after it was erected to commemorate
the first Soviet cosmonaut*

At the starting line of the hundred metre
sprint. On your Marx …
*English graffito at Cosmos Hotel quarters
for athletes taking part in 1980 Olympics*

Russian roulette for women: six birth
control pills — one of them is an aspirin.

STUPID IDIOTS! YOU COME HERE AND
WRITE CRAP ALL OVER THE WALLS.
*written in huge letters over a
graffiti-covered lavatory wall,
in Moscow*

People who write upon these walls
 Often write naughty words like 'balls' —
Come on, folks, enough's enough,
 Can't you write some other stuff?

Erith, Kent

NEVER CARRY YOUR LUGGAGE IN
JAPANESE HOTELS — LET YELLOW PAGES
DO THE WALKING.

Exeter

THE DEVIL MAKES WORK FOR IDLE
HANDS TO DO.
— Give me his address.

*quoted in newspaper for the
unemployed, 1983*

E VEN YOSSER WOULDN'T WANT THIS
JOB.

in dust on lorry on A606, 1983

S he was only the roadmaker's daughter but
she liked her asphalt.

Taunton

I 'm into wife-swapping. I will accept *anything*
in exchange.

Hastings

J at bewust
[Shoplift wisely.]

Nijmegen, The Netherlands

GOD IS ALIVE. SPEAK TO HIM.
— it's cheaper after six.

loo, Sydney Opera House

The population explosion started with a bang.

Skegness

FREE LECH WALESA
— Swap him for Arthur Scargill.

on tailboard of lorry, seen at Heywood, Lancs.

Derek ******* sucks farts out of dead seagulls in Argyle Street.

Glasgow University Students' Union

Did you know the lightest thing on earth is your penis? Even imagination can lift it.

Did you know the heaviest thing on earth is a shit? Even Samson had to drop it.

Did you know the sharpest thing on earth is a fart? It can go through your trousers without tearing them.

gents' loo, Dundee, 1962

As I sit here amidst this wit
I think Rabbie Burns must have come to shit.
And judging by the fucking smell
I think he must have brought his horse as well.

gents' loo, Elie, Fife, 1962

Did you know that the best Post Impressionists were Poles?

London W11

Women Against Racism

— Say yes,

Leeds

Avoid Hangovers – Stay Drunk.
Billingsgate, London

What on earth is ontology?
— What in heaven's name is metaphysics?
— What the hell is Christianity about?
— What the deuce is tennis?
— What the fuck is sexology?
— Now look here, I mean, bloddy hell, you stupid ignorant fucker, you have lowered the tone of this intellectual game!

Klagenfurt, Austria

Unemployment isn't working!
Grafton, Auckland, New Zealand

HELP CND—BLOW YOURSELF UP.
Oxford

Grow your own dope. Plant a Pom.
Carlton, Vic.

FUMA BENE
FUMA SANO
FUMA SOLO PAKISTANO.
[Smoke well, smoke healthily, smoke only
Pakistani.]
railway station, Treviso, Italy

JUDAISM RULES OY VEY?

school, Johannesburg, South Africa

Dudley Moore is a phallic thimble.

London W1

I hope I look as good as Joan Collins when I get to her age.

ladies' loo, Eastbourne

Mummy, mummy, what's an orgasm? — I dunno, ask your father.

Chester

2.30 Time to go to Chinese dentist.

Greenwich, London

Isaac Newton didn't discover gravity. He invented heavier-than-air apples.

motorway service area on M1

Dominus illuminatio mea

on generator outside Balliol College, Oxford, during Three Day Week, 1974

Children in the front seat cause accidents. Accidents in the back seat cause children.

girls' loo, Penrose High School, Auckland, New Zealand

BRING YOUR DOUBTS
— And have them confirmed.

addition to poster advertising
evangelist Luis Palau's London
meetings, 1984

There's one born again every minute.

ditto.

I thought Midge Ure was an insect-repellent
until I discovered Smirnoff.

London W2

Up with dresses, down with pants.

Alloa

The Argentinians gave Galtieri a glass-bottomed boat so that he could see his Air Force.

gents' loo, Bristol

That's another fine mess you've got me into, Stanley.

Port Stanley, Falkland Islands, 1982

I wrote the Hitler diary!

US, 1983

My mum says if I'm not in bed by 10.30, I'm to come home.

Stirling

addition to traffic sign, Western Australia

IS MUFFIN THE MULE A SEXUAL OFFENCE?
— No, but Dobbin the Horse might be.
Catworth, Cambs.

I'm into B & D (boozing and drinking).

Manchester

Australians are living proof that aborigines screw kangaroos.

'The Old China Hand' pub, Wanchai,
Hong Kong

I thought Muhammad Ali was a street in Cairo until I discovered Smirnoff.

Leeds

Mission impossible — Maidenhead revisited.

Woodford Green

FLOG MUGGERS
— Mug floggers.

Hampstead Underground station,
London

Bestiality is beastly boring
Adultery is doubly boring
Deflowering is bloody boring
Lesbianism isn't at all boring.

Klagenfurt, Austria

A tired old fairy from Rome
Took a leprechaun back to his home.
As he entered the elf
He said to himself
I'd be much better off in a gnome.

traditional

FREE THE GRECIAN 2000.

Brighton

WOMEN LIKE THE SIMPLE THINGS
IN LIFE — LIKE MEN
— Simple things please simple minds.

Exeter

If undertakers were nationalised, then
everyone could have a State funeral.

Liverpool Street station, London

May Graffiti never fade

Alloa

Also by Nigel Rees in
Unwin Paperbacks

GRAFFITI 1, 2, 3 & 4

'a flashing delight of wit, simple bawdiness, social comment and piercing common sense'
Sunday Express

'a devastating harvest of mural comment'
The Evening News

'Gems must be preserved for posterity'
Woman's World

'a special art form'

Liverpool Post

BABES & SUCKLINGS

In this book Nigel Rees presents a selection of actual junior *bons mots*, a child's eye view of such grown-up matters as sex, religion and life in general. BABES AND SUCKLINGS is a delightful and touching view of parents, pets, Royalty and breast-feeding as they appear to those who are quite obviously young enough to know better.

QUOTE ... UNQUOTE

Aphorisms and apothegms, *bons mots* and bromides, epigrams and epitaphs, repartees and rejoinders, squibs and squelches, wise saws and wisecracks — that is the stuff Nigel Rees' radio series 'Quote ... Unquote' is made of. Part quiz, part anthology, the 'Quote ... Unquote' book deliciously captures its flavour.

There are catchphrases and spoonerisms, famous first and last words. Sam Goldwynisms, Dorothy Parkerisms, Margot Asquith's brilliant 'margots' and the gaffes, goofs, immortal and mortal remarks of Prime Ministers, Presidents, film, radio and TV stars, and all sorts of other people.

QUOTE ... UNQUOTE 2

'Messing about with quotations' is how Nigel Rees describes this second collection of quotes and quizzes from the popular radio series. This new compendium contains the immortal musings of kings, presidents and menu-writers, legendary crossword clues, hilarious newspaper headlines and rare jokes from the Bible. A host of steamy sayings proves there's more to sex than just doing it.

QUOTE ... UNQUOTE 3

It's amazing what people do with quotations. Agatha Christie murdered them, Bertie Wooster mangled them, Margaret Thatcher and Ronald Reagan spout them and Nigel Rees collects them ...

In this third book he has gathered together an entertaining pot-pourri of verbal lore including many marvellous quotes you won't find in any ordinary dictionary or anthology of quotations.

'Quote—Unquote 3' pays special attention to Anon (that prolific minter of quotable quotes), sentiments that could have been better expressed in graveyards, unbelievable but real book titles, and household names that accompany some rather less than household faces.

QUOTABLE TRIVIA

Forty sparkling quizzes on the most trivial aspects of quotations. Designed to delight, bemuse and bewilder, QUOTABLE TRIVIA is a quiz-book in which the answers are infinitely more interesting than the questions! What's more, the daftest answers are usually the right ones!

Also available:

SHOWBIZ TRIVIA
SIXTIES TRIVIA

Also by Nigel Rees

Babes & Sucklings	£1.50 ☐
Graffiti 1	£1.50 ☐
Graffiti 2	£1.50 ☐
Graffiti 3	£1.50 ☐
Graffiti 4	£1.50 ☐
Quote … Unquote	£1.50 ☐
Quote … Unquote 2	£1.50 ☐
Quote … Unquote 3	£1.50 ☐
Quotable Trivia	£1.75 ☐
Showbiz Trivia	£1.75 ☐
Sixties Trivia	£1.75 ☐

All these books are available at your local bookshop or newsagent, or can be ordered direct by post. Just tick the titles you want and fill in the form below.

Name ....

Address ....

....

....

Write to Unwin Cash Sales, PO Box 11, Falmouth, Cornwall TR10 9EN.

Please enclose remittance to the value of the cover price plus:

UK: 55p for the first book plus 22p for the second book, thereafter 14p for each additional book ordered to a maximum charge of £1.75.

BFPO and EIRE: 55p for the first book plus 22p for the second book and 14p for the next 7 books and thereafter 8p per book.

OVERSEAS: £1.00 for the first book plus 25p per copy for each additional book.

Unwin Paperbacks reserve the right to show new retail prices on covers, which may differ from those previously advertised in the text or elsewhere. Postage rates are also subject to revision.